John Ware

Ian Hundey

Fitzhenry & Whiteside

Contents

THE CANADIANS®
A Continuing Series

John Ware

Author: Ian Hundey
Cover Illustration: John Mardon
Design: Kerry Designs

THE CANADIANS® *is a registered trademark of Fitzhenry & Whiteside Limited.*

For Chris, a new Albertan, and Caitlyn, the newest Hundey

Fitzhenry & Whiteside acknowledges with thanks the Canada Council for the Arts, and the Ontario Arts Council for their support of our publishing program. We acknowledge the financial support of the Government of Canada through the Book Publishing Industry Development Program (BPIDP) for our publishing activities.

Canada Council   Conseil des Arts
for the Arts   du Canada

ONTARIO ARTS COUNCIL
CONSEIL DES ARTS DE L'ONTARIO

Library and Archives Canada Cataloguing in Publication
Hundey, Ian, 1945-
John Ware / Ian Hundey.
(The Canadians)
Includes index.
ISBN 1-55041-872-6

1. Ware, John, 1845?-1905—Juvenile literature. 2. Cowboys—Alberta—Biography—Juvenile literature.
3. Ranchers—Alberta—Biography—Juvenile literature. 4. Black Canadians—Alberta—Biography—Juvenile literature.
I. Title. II. Series: Canadians

FC3217.1.W3H85 2005   j971.23'02'092   C2005-905822-6

No part of this publication may be reproduced in any form, by any means, without permission in writing from the publisher.

Printed and bound in Canada.
ISBN 1-55041-872-6

© 2006 Fitzhenry & Whiteside Limited
195 Allstate Parkway, Markham, Ontario L3R 4T8

Prologue
The Days of John Ware

John Ware stands tall in the history of Alberta. An ex-slave from the American South, John rode into Alberta in 1882—the same year that the Canadian government made Alberta a separate district in the North-West Territories. John died in 1905, less than two weeks after Alberta became a province.

Over those 23 years, John lived through key changes in Alberta's early history. He helped drive one of the first large cattle herds onto the open range, where the buffalo had been king only a few years before. In the 1880s he worked as a cowboy for two of the largest ranch companies. He knew many of the powerful cattle barons and had won their respect.

In the 1890s John left the ranch companies just before they went into decline. At Sheep Creek, he started his own ranch. It was one of the first small, family-run ranches that sprouted across the District of Alberta. In 1900 John saw homesteaders' fences carving up the last of the open range in southern Alberta. So he and his family moved north and started another ranch on the Red Deer River near Brooks.

As an Alberta cowboy and rancher, John Ware survived stampedes, blizzards, rustlers, and racism. Known for being dependable, determined, honest, and good-natured, John reflected the best traits of self-reliant ranchers and cowboys. Throughout his life, John was famous for his cowboy skills, especially bronc riding. He rode broncs and roped steers in informal cowboy contests—the forerunners of the western rodeo. Yet as the rodeo's popularity climbed, the cowboy life that John knew was vanishing.

The year 1905 marked the start of a new Alberta. In the new province, farmers, townspeople, oil workers, and others would shape society. But Alberta's roots run directly back to the days of the open range and the early cattle ranches—back to the days of John Ware.

Chapter 1
From Slave to Cowboy

It was lonely rounding up strays on the Alberta range in 1883. John Ware had plenty of time to think back. What a long and strange trail he had ridden. The cattle drive of 1882 from Idaho to Canada had been a great adventure. John had faced both stampedes and cattle rustlers on that trip.

There were other adventures that stretched even further back—the gold rush in Montana, the cattle drive from Texas. But John's life had started in an even more distant place. "You've come a long way, John," he thought to himself. For John Ware had been born a slave in the southern United States.

Slaves had no birth certificates, and none of John's family could read or write, so there were no records to mark his entry into the world. John was unsure about his exact date of birth, but thought it might have been in 1845.

John grew up on a plantation near Georgetown, South Carolina. He lived with his parents and ten sisters and brothers in a small, dirt-floored cabin. The crude housing for slaves was often lined up in tight rows in a separate compound. That made it easier for the plantation's overseer to keep a close watch.

John and his family, like all slaves in the American South, were the property of their owners. Slaves had no civil rights or protection under the law. They were captive labour who planted, tended, and harvested the cotton, rice, and other crops that fed the economy of the southern United States. In return, their owners provided the slaves with the barest of life's necessities. John and his family probably consumed a diet based on rice or cornmeal with some molasses for taste. Occasionally there was meat, but always the cheapest cuts. On such rations, slaves worked in the fields from dawn to dusk.

Always big for his age, John Ware probably took his place among the other field hands when he was just a young boy. Most children started to work in the fields when they were

seven or eight, or even younger. Like the adults, they were expected to put in long days planting, weeding, and harvesting under the hot southern sun.

Slaves—men, women, and children—in front of their living quarters, South Carolina, 1862.

John Ware never went to school. No slaves did. Most slave owners felt that slaves were incapable of learning. Others worried that if slaves became educated they might learn dangerous ideas and think about bettering themselves. John must have wished he had learned to read and to write more than just his own name.

But John learned other lessons on the Georgetown plantation. His master sometimes forced young slaves to fight as entertainment for his guests. One time the master staged a survivor contest. The last boy standing would receive a prize of a pair of shoes. The final fight came down to John and a smaller boy. It was clear that John was bigger and stronger. Yet it was the smaller boy who floored John with one innocent-looking blow. The winner took his prize and was congratulated by John, who had let the smaller boy win. John had never worn shoes in his life and saw that the prized shoes would not fit him. John also remembered that the smaller boy's mother had cared for his own mother when she was ill. Young John was already showing that he had a generous spirit.

A copy of the Emancipation Proclamation with a portrait of President Lincoln, who pushed for the abolition of slavery.

John needed a strong spirit to survive the cruelty that surrounded him every day. One time John was severely whipped after he stopped his master from beating another slave. But the worst punishment was reserved for slaves who tried to escape, something John witnessed firsthand. Two runaway slaves were captured as they were fleeing north. When the men were brought back, they were placed in stocks for three hours beneath a blazing sun. Then they were tied to a rack and their bodies stretched. John must have felt their incredible pain and suffering. Knowing that similar punishment awaited any slave who sought freedom, he held little hope of escaping his life of slavery.

John saw his fortunes change dramatically on January 1, 1863. That was the day President Abraham Lincoln issued the Emancipation Proclamation, which declared that "all persons held as slaves shall be free." However, few slaves were freed until the Civil War ended in 1865.

In 1865 John was 20 years old—and free for the first time in his life. He decided to leave South Carolina and seek his fortune in the American West. But first he had a score to settle with the plantation owner. Just before John left, he collared the man and marched him to the whipping tree. There was no doubt that the strapping young man could deliver whatever punishment he chose. As a boy, John had been forced to fight other young slaves. Should he now use his fists on his ex-master? Maybe he should whip the former slave owner as revenge for his own whipping. John chose neither. Rather, he chose to be a better man than his ex-master. John walked away from his former owner and took his first steps towards a new life.

Leaving behind both the South and his family, John headed west. He didn't know much about the western United States, but he knew it was horse country. A love of horses was one thing that John took with him from his days as a slave. Now that he was free, maybe he could find work on a horse ranch in the Wild West.

By heading west, John was part of a migration of Americans looking for adventure and a new start after the Civil War. Many

From Slave to Cowboy

migrants were former slaves who wanted to put the South far behind them. Some went only as far as the midwestern states, like Kansas. Others went further west to horse and cattle country in the state of Texas or northwest to the new American territories of Wyoming, Dakota, Montana, and Idaho.

John set out for Texas. On his way he probably crossed paths with other freed slaves who had joined cavalry units in the West. The Native people called them "Buffalo Soldiers." In Texas, Buffalo Soldiers helped protect wagon trains, survey parties, railway crews, and cattle ranchers. They built forts, roads, and telegraph lines. They also fought in the Indian Wars in the 1860s and 1870s.

When some Buffalo Soldiers retired, they turned to a new occupation. They became cowboys. One of the most famous cowboys was Nat Love, a former slave from Tennessee. Throughout cattle country, he became known as Deadwood Dick after beating all the other cowboys in riding and shooting contests in Deadwood City, Dakota Territory. Not all cowboys were as famous as Deadwood Dick, but many lived exciting lives, driving cattle and breaking horses across the Wild West.

The cowboy life appealed to young John Ware. It was full of adventure and independence—and horses. By the 1870s John was working on a horse ranch near Fort Worth, Texas. His job was halter-breaking colts—the first step in training a horse—and he was very good at it. After watching other cowboys breaking horses, he asked if he could try. John was fearless

A cowboy camp during a cattle drive in Montana, about 1890.

when he mounted his first wild horse. He managed to stay on while the horse bucked and reared and then jumped over the corral fence and galloped out of sight. When horse and rider returned, John was still in the saddle and the horse was under control. It didn't take long for John to gain a reputation in Fort Worth as a skilled horseman.

Texas could not contain John, however. In the 1870s there was a boom in the American cattle industry. American railways were

Cattle on the range in Montana Territory, about 1880.

pushing west, and ambitious cattle-men were driving herds to rail-heads in Missouri and Kansas. Trains carried thousands of cattle east to feed the swelling American population in towns and cities. At the same time, herds were being driven from Texas north and west into new grazing lands in Wyoming, Dakota, Idaho, and Montana. For a skilled horseman like John Ware, there were plenty of opportunities to sign on with an outfit driving cattle up the Texas Trail and into Montana Territory.

In 1879 John joined a cattle drive on the Texas Trail. He was one of a dozen cowboys hired to herd 2,000 head of Texas cattle and a string of saddle horses northwest into Montana. John knew horses, but he was a greenhorn on a cattle drive—and the only Black man. John ended up with the job of drag-man, riding all day at the tail of the herd, breathing dust and wiping dirt from his eyes. By the time the outfit reached Montana, John had learned to round up strays, turn stampedes, and drive reluctant cattle across rivers. And he had ridden the meanest horses in the ramuda—the outfit's string of saddle horses. John Ware had proved himself as a cowboy.

In Montana, John was lured away from cowboy life when

Gold rush towns provided some of the first markets for western cattle. Cowboys drive cattle into Barkerville, British Columbia, in 1868.

he caught a dose of gold fever. He travelled to the mountains near Virginia City, Nevada, in search of riches. Like other gold rush hopefuls, John failed to make his fortune. He decided that horses and cattle were more depend-able than gold and began the long journey back to Texas.

In Idaho Territory in early 1882, John hooked up

From Slave to Cowboy

with Bill Moodie, a cowboy he had befriended on the Montana cattle drive. Then Tom Lynch appeared on the scene. He was looking for experienced cowboys to drive cattle into the District of Alberta in the North-West Territories.

First Nations hunted buffalo by driving them over a buffalo jump. Over the centuries, these hunters killed thousands of buffalo. In a few decades, commercial hunters killed millions. (Library and Archives Canada. Acc. No. 1946-110-1. Gift of Mrs. J.B. Jardine.)

In 1882 the District of Alberta was a brand new piece of Canada. It had just been created as part of the North-West Territories. The government of Canada had purchased these vast territories—originally called Rupert's Land—from the Hudson's Bay Company in 1870.

In 1870 the southern part of the North-West Territories was wide-open prairie, home to Native people and Métis—and huge herds of buffalo. For generations, First Nations families had been hunting the buffalo and using it like a sort of general store. Buffalo meat and pemmican were staples of their diet. Bladders and bones were made into utensils and tools. Hides were turned into shelter, clothes, and blankets, or handed over to fur traders in exchange for manufactured goods like cloth, iron pots, guns, and ammunition.

A lot changed between 1870 and 1882, when John Ware first rode into the new District of Alberta. In 1874 the North-West Mounted Police (NWMP) set up headquarters at Fort Macleod to maintain law and order and to establish Canada's control over the territories. In 1877 the Canadian government

Estimates of the number of buffalo killed between 1830 and 1880 range up to a high of 40 million. Buffalo pelts were used for coats and robes, the hides for industrial machine-belts, and the bones for fertilizer.

convinced the Blackfoot, Blood, Piegan, Sarcee, and Stoney First Nations to sign Treaty Number 7. Under the treaty, the Native people agreed to give up claims to their traditional hunting lands and to settle on government reserves. In return, the government promised to provide them with annual payments and agricultural implements.

The biggest change during those years was in the size of the buffalo herds. The huge herds had completely vanished, and it seemed as if it had happened almost overnight. In 1877 the Chief Factor of the Hudson's Bay Company reported seeing one herd that covered the open range from east of Calgary to as far as the eye could see. Just a few years later, Canada's Governor General wrote: "Throughout this country we saw, in 1881, the dung of buffalo, although we only met a small herd of thirteen bulls." Everywhere on the Great Plains of western Canada and the U.S., there were piles of buffalo bones but almost no buffalo.

As the buffalo disappeared, Native people on the reserves started getting desperate for food. Some resorted to snaring gophers and butchering stray cattle. The Canadian government stepped in to supply beef for the reserves.

At first the I.G. Baker Company and the T. C. Power Company of Montana brought in American beef, but the Canadian government was not happy with this arrangement. It had no interest in making Montana companies rich. Nor did it want to leave the success of its treaties with the First Nations in American hands. The federal government wanted Canadian beef suppliers. That meant developing a cattle industry in places like the District of Alberta.

In the 1870s there were some cattle and the bare beginnings of a cattle industry in the district. The first small herd was imported by a missionary on the Bow River in 1873. The mission brought in a larger herd from Montana in 1874. That was the year that the North-West Mounted Police (NWMP) arrived in Fort Macleod, bringing with them over 200 head of cattle. In 1878 some policemen retired and turned to a new career in the cattle business.

In 1879 two government cattle ranches were established, one near Calgary at Fish Creek and the other at Pincher Creek. By the summer there were more than 1,000 head of cattle in the area. But this number fell far short of what was needed for the NWMP posts and the reserves. The Native people were now desperately short of food. The Canadian government needed to do much more—and quickly—to get a cattle industry up and running.

Investors from eastern Canada and Britain were already eyeing the lush grass-lands that spread across the plains and foothills of the Rockies. For them, the open range looked like a land of opportunity for anyone with enough money to get into the cattle business in a big way. They saw the Native reserves and NWMP posts as ready markets. And they knew that new markets would open up as the Canadian Pacific Railway pushed further west, bringing new immigrants and settlers to the prairies.

Robert Patterson was one of the NWMP who became a rancher in Alberta after his discharge in 1878.

Powerful business voices started lobbying Prime Minister John A. Macdonald to do something to encourage investors to start up cattle ranches in the West. For his part, the prime minister was ready to act. He wanted to secure the West for Canada, and one way was to divert investment in the cattle industry from the United States to the North-West Territories. Macdonald was also aware of the plight of the Native people on the reserves, and he needed to justify the noble, but expensive, decision to build a transcontinental railway.

In 1881 Macdonald's Conservative government set up a land-leasing system that offered ranchers grazing leases of up to 100,000 acres (about 40,000 hectares) at the rate of only one

In 1882 Fred Stimson established the North-West Cattle Company at the Bar U Ranch, one of the largest and most successful ranches in the District of Alberta.

cent per acre for 21 years. The lease-holder had to stock the land with one head for every 10 acres (4 hectares). That meant 10,000 head of cattle if the maximum acreage was leased.

The impact of this leasing system was dramatic. Wealthy investors started setting up large ranches and importing big herds of cattle. Imports of cattle rose from 1,352 head in 1880 to 6,284 in 1881. By 1882 cattle imports had shot up to 16,282 head.

One of the first big cattle businesses in the District of Alberta was the North-West Cattle Company. It was started by Fred Stimson, a wealthy cattle and horse farmer from Quebec. Set-up costs were high—about $150,000 (more than $3 million in today's dollars). That much was needed to lease grazing land from the government, buy cattle, put up ranch buildings, and hire cowboys. Stimson needed investors, so he approached the Allan family, owners of Canada's biggest shipping line. The Allan family immediately agreed to invest in Stimson's cattle venture. It was a good business decision: western beef transported by rail to the St. Lawrence River could be shipped by the Allan Line to Britain and other European markets.

Stimson retained a share of the ownership and was also appointed company manager. He travelled west and chose a ranch site at Pekisko Creek on the grazing range south of Calgary and west of High River. The ranch was named the Bar U after the cattle brand that the North-West Company had registered with the territorial government.

Stimson was an experienced stockman when it came to eastern cattle. But he was no cowboy and knew little about western herds. So he hired Tom Lynch, an experienced cattle drover. Lynch had been born in Idaho and had spent most of his life driving cattle, first from Oregon and Washington into Wyoming and Montana. Then he had driven one of the first big herds from Montana to the North-West Mounted Police posts in the District of Alberta.

In 1882 Lynch and Stimson travelled south to Idaho to buy cattle to stock the new Bar U Ranch. They purchased 3,000 prime cattle and 75 horses. While Stimson returned to the Bar U, Lynch set about hiring a crew for the long cattle drive into Canada. Lynch was looking for experienced cowhands, and his search led him to Bill Moodie. Moodie was interested, but only if Lynch would hire his friend John Ware.

As soon as he was hired, John found he had to prove himself again. On the first day of the drive, Lynch gave John a broken-down horse with a battered saddle and assigned him the job of nighthawk. That meant John would be patrolling the cattle all night—one of the worst jobs on a cattle drive.

Like this cowboy, John Ware learned how wild a bronc could be.

After a few nights, John asked Lynch for a better saddle. In return, he was willing to ride a horse that was harder to handle. Lynch offered John a better saddle—if he could ride one of the outfit's most rebellious horses. When it came time for John to mount the horse, all the other cowboys circled round to watch. The horse was snorting, but John was calm as he approached the beast. As soon as he was in the saddle, the horse reared up trying to unseat its rider. The cowboys hooted as the horse bucked and twirled. But John rode the wicked mustang "from ears to tail" until the horse gave up the fight.

John rode back to the circle of cowboys, who were impressed by his display of horsemanship. John declared to Tom Lynch that he was happy with the horse. And Lynch gave John a better saddle.

Within a few days, John had more than proven himself to Lynch and the other cowboys. He was one of the best hands at keeping the herd moving and rounding up strays. And he could handle any horse in the remuda. Tom Lynch promoted John to the day shift and told him to ride near the front of the herd.

And so John settled into the daily life of a cowboy. For

Main Street, Fort Macleod, 1880s.

more than four months, he and the other cowboys rose at sunrise, ate breakfast, and then mounted their horses. They broke at noon to let the cattle graze, and then got them moving again until they stopped for the night. Each day's routine brought John and his fellow cowboys about 15 to 20 kilometres closer to the District of Alberta.

Sometimes the routine was broken by a stampede or the need to round up strays. In Montana, John had some trouble with rustlers. He stumbled upon two cowboys branding cattle in a temporary corral. The men looked suspicious and the cows looked familiar. As John rode closer, the men appeared ready to draw their guns. John rode his horse into the cowboys and knocked them to the ground. Then he slipped from the saddle, grabbed their revolvers, and tied them up. John drove the stolen cattle and the rustlers back to camp. Often rustlers were given frontier justice on the spot. But this time the trail crew let them go—without their horses and guns.

In September 1882, after a drive of about 1,200 kilometres, John Ware reached the Bar U Ranch at the head of the herd. The cattle were in remarkable condition considering the length of their journey. The *Macleod Gazette* observed: "This is evidently one of the most successful drives ever made to this country." Wild celebrations in the Macleod Hotel marked the arrival of the cowboys and the new herd at Bar U Ranch.

John Ware had found his new home. A man who had spent his youth as a slave was now an expert horseman and respected cattle driver. At the age of 37, John settled in to his new life as an Alberta cowboy.

Chapter 2
Cowboy Life in Early Alberta

In the fall of 1882 Fred Stimson paid off the cowboys who had driven the ranch's herd from Idaho. When Stimson handed over John Ware's pay, he asked him to stay on as a permanent ranch hand. As a good judge of men—and a good businessman—Stimson knew the value of keeping a man like John. Trail boss Tom Lynch had told Stimson that John was one of the best men in the outfit. He was an expert at handling cattle and horses—and rustlers. He was dependable and sober. And he was well liked and respected by all his companions on the trail.

John accepted Fred Stimson's offer, with one condition. He remembered his debt to Bill Moodie, and declared that he would stay only if his friend Bill Moodie was taken on. Moodie was happy to remain with his trail partner. And Stimson was happy to gain two good cowhands. Most of the American cowboys who had been on the cattle drive headed home. But John Ware and Bill Moodie settled in to work for the North-West Cattle Company at the Bar U Ranch in the new District of Alberta.

John was impressed by Alberta. The grazing lands were full of grasses as lush as any he had seen in the U.S. He saw how the North-West Mounted Police had brought law and order to the area. He heard about the treaties that had been signed with the First Nations. John had lived through the violence of the Civil War. He had seen even more violence in the lawlessness and Indian Wars of the American West. In this more peaceful land, he saw steady work for an experienced cowboy. Here was a place where a cowboy might save up a stake and start his own ranch.

When they moved into the Bar U's bunkhouse, John and Bill Moodie didn't have a lot of unpacking to do. Cowboys travelled light. Most days John wore a battered hat, an old coat, a vest, a flannel shirt, thick trousers with wide leather belt, high boots,

Cowboys in their working clothes in the 1880s.

The Bar U's second bunk-house is the building on the right. The pile of firewood provided fuel for both heating and cooking.

and a wide-brimmed hat to protect him from the sun and rain. Some cowboys wore leather chaps to protect their legs. (Fancy sheepskin chaps were reserved for posed studio portraits.) Like all cowboys, John wore a bandana, which he pulled around his face to keep out dust and cold. In winter some cowboys wore heavy winter coats, while others faced the bitter cold and biting wind on the open range by wrapping themselves in a blanket.

John carried a revolver, which he stuck in his belt or his chaps. More important than his revolver were the tools of the cowboy's trade: his lariat, quirt (a short whip with a stout leather handle), bridle, and saddle.

When John and Bill Moodie moved in, there was nothing fancy about the bunkhouse at the Bar U. It was a low, long building made of cottonwood logs with big gaps between them. The floor was dirt and the roof was made of sod. There was a fireplace at one end and rows of sleeping bunks along one wall. Buckets and basins were set out for washing and shaving. In 1882 the bunkhouse was home to only six cowboys. But as the Bar U grew, the old bunkhouse was replaced by a larger building that was a combination of cowboy cookhouse and bunkhouse. The cook stove, pantry, and dining table were on the main floor. In the loft were sleeping quarters for the cowboys.

A cowboy gets ready to brand as two heelers tighten the ropes on another steer.

John's working day started with breakfast at 5:00 a.m. Bacon was the staple dish, often served with soda bread. The outfit's cook was used to hungry cowboys, but feeding John Ware was a real challenge. For breakfast John ate as much food as two men and needed sandwiches as big as Bibles for lunch.

There was plenty to do as the Bar U Ranch began its operations in the fall of 1882. The first job for John and the other ranch hands was branding the herd they had driven up from Idaho. Since these were full-grown cattle, it took at least five men to do the branding. Two cowboys on horseback lassoed the front and rear legs of the cow or steer. Then two cowboys wrestled the animal to the ground while two heelers kept the ropes tight. Finally, another cowboy pressed a heated branding iron into its flank.

When the cattle were all marked with the Bar U brand, John started to work with the ranch's horses. Every ranch had a supply of horses for cattle drives and round-ups and for riding trail on grazing herds. Cowboys rode range horses, sometimes called cayuses. Bred from wild stock, cayuses were small, compact, and tough—well suited to the western climate and terrain. Some were wild horses that had been captured on the range. Cowboys called them "broncos" or "broncs."

Breaking broncs was one of John's favourite jobs. On all the big ranches in the District of Alberta, John and other courageous cowboys broke horses to saddle for the North-West Mounted Police, local settlers, and townspeople. They also had to provide themselves with a supply of horses for trail drives and round-ups.

These cowboys are catching their mounts from the remuda, a string of horses ridden in the round-up.

Breaking broncs was a dangerous job. "After you have been on a few minutes," one cowboy wrote, "you don't know which is your head and which your heels, or what your name is, or how old you are. All you feel is an indistinct impression that one end of your spine is sticking out about four inches and bumping against the saddle, and that the other is sticking about the same distance into your brain and is working about in there."

John Ware was good at breaking broncs. It took skill, strength, and timing. John also relied on his understanding of horse behaviour and his own determination. Sometimes he would get the horse's attention by grabbing it by the ear and using his strength to make it stand still. Other times he roped the bronc and used his strong arms and weight to bring it under control as it circled the corral. Then he mounted the horse, tightened his long, powerful legs around its girth, and gave the horse its head. Often it galloped off with John jerking and swaying in the saddle. Eventually the horse exhausted itself and realized that it was not going to throw this immovable man from its back. John had won again.

Another big part of John's job at the Bar U was riding herd. Along with other cowboys, he patrolled the open range to check on cattle grazing on the North-West Cattle Company lease. Besides keeping watch on the herd, the Bar U crew had to make sure that their cattle didn't mix with other herds. Not long after the cattle were settled on the Bar U lease, another herd was driven past on a nearby trail. The cattle were headed for the Cochrane Ranche at the Big Hill range west of Calgary. There would be utter confusion if the thousands of cows from the two ranching companies intermingled. But John and the Bar U crew managed to keep their stock away from the Cochrane herd.

With the Bar U herd intact, John and the other cowboys headed back to the ranch. It was still early in October, but already a light snow was falling on the open range. Suddenly a

ferocious blizzard hit. The snow increased and a north wind began to howl. The cattle sensed that the only relief from this bitter weather lay on their home range in Idaho. So they turned their backs to the wind and began to drift south. The Bar U cowboys rode out to turn the cattle, but the herd instinct had taken over. By nightfall the blizzard had not let up and the cattle were still on the move. The ranch hands returned to the Bar U to wait out the storm. One cowboy, however, did not return. It was John Ware.

After this round-up in 1893, the cattle that were to be sold were herded into the home ranch's corral.

The storm raged for three days. When it ended, the Bar U cowboys went searching for John and the herd. Perhaps John had taken shelter in the log shack at the Bar U's upper camp, west of the main ranch. But there was no sign of him there. For a full day the cowboys rode south, pushing their way through heavy snowdrifts. They found a few lone cows, but no sign of the main herd—or of John.

Then Bill Moodie got a report from the Fort Macleod stagecoach driver. Cattle and a solitary rider had been spotted further south. The searchers forged southward for another full day. As they rode through grasslands that had only a dusting of snow, they saw a fresh trail made by a cattle herd. Finally at nightfall they saw a campfire, a huddled figure, and cattle—lots of cattle. They approached carefully, in case he turned out to be a cattle thief. The figure rose to his feet, and it was clear from his size that it was John Ware.

As the men warmed themselves by the fire, John told his

Winters in Alberta could be hard on cattle on the open range.

story. He had tried to force one wing of the herd to circle. But it was a futile tactic. So he let the cattle head south and tried to keep the herd together. For almost two days, he stayed in the saddle with the moving herd. The cattle were exhausted and stopped to rest. But the blizzard was relentless. Soon the herd was on the move again. Finally on the fourth day the cattle found grass that was not covered with snow. As the herd grazed, John managed to shoot a deer, start a fire, and eat. He had not been dressed for a winter blizzard and admitted that he had been cold. John joked that he had been so cold that he was afraid to flex his fingers in case they broke off like icicles.

By letting the cattle drift until they found grass, John had saved the Bar U herd. The cattle had travelled about 70 kilometres from the Bar U range and ended up on the south bank of the Oldman River. With winter settling in further north, Fred Stimson decided to leave the herd there to graze for the winter. It was a wise decision. The Cochrane herd had been caught in the same blizzard and had also drifted south looking for grass and shelter. When the herd was finally located, the Cochrane ranch manager ordered the cowboys to drive the cattle back to the main ranch. There the exhausted animals found the grazing lands still covered with ice-crusted snow. The Cochrane Ranche ended up losing 3,000 head of cattle.

In 1882, when John arrived in the District of Alberta, the range was entirely open. There was not a fence between Fort Macleod and the outskirts of Calgary. Cattle grazed freely on the lands leased by the large ranching companies. Twice a year they had to be rounded up. In the fall, cowboys rounded up the cattle that were ready to be sold. The rest of the herd was left on the range to graze over the winter. In May or June, it was time for spring round-up. Cowboys searched for the cattle that had survived the winter. They separated their stock from cattle from other ranches and branded the calves that had been born on the range.

John took part in the Bar U's first round-up in May 1883. The grasslands that had been covered by snow and ice in the great blizzard were now green with spring grasses and dotted with wildflowers. When they reached the herd, the Bar U cowboys set up their camp on the bank of the Oldman River. Here they corralled their horses and the cook set up the chuckwagon.

John revelled in round-up life. He enjoyed being outdoors for days on end and sleeping under the stars. He rode endless hours without tiring and with great skill. That skill was never more evident than the day the other cowboys thought John would surely die.

The cowboys were having trouble with an unruly horse and asked for John's help. John mounted the horse in his usual confident way. He stayed on as the horse reared, but then it galloped off towards the Oldman River. At break-neck speed the horse launched itself over the bank and plunged into deep water. The other cowboys held their breath until the horse finally emerged downstream—with John still firmly on its back.

Around the campfire that night, everyone listened to stories about John's wild ride. There were always stories around the campfire, as well as other tomfoolery. Cowboys were renowned for

This round-up cook has spread out his supplies and set up his stove in a cook tent. The chuckwagon that carried all of his kitchen necessities is visible through the open rear flap.

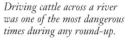

Driving cattle across a river was one of the most dangerous times during any round-up.

their practical jokes, and John played more than a few. No one forgot the one time that John was the butt of a practical joke that backfired. Everyone at the Bar U knew about John's fear of snakes. One night his Bar U mates slipped a rope in his bedroll. When John slid inside, his feet felt a long, thin object. Then one of the cowboys twitched the rope. John leapt to his feet and hopped madly about—to the great delight of the other cowboys.

John was normally even-tempered, but he was upset by this prank. He also missed his friend Bill Moodie. Bill had left the Bar U in the early spring, for a reason only a cowboy would understand. Fred Stimson had given Bill the job of cutting some trees for corral poles. Moodie remarked that there was no Bar U horse gentle enough for the job. Puzzled, Stimson asked why he needed a horse at all. To that Bill replied, "If I can't do the job on a horse, I can't do it." Moodie turned his horse south and rode back across the border. He never returned. John thought it was a good time to take a break from cowboy life.

In the summer of 1883, John took a job digging irrigation ditches at a crossing of the Highwood River where settlers had built a store and trading post. His co-worker was Dan Riley, a young migrant from Prince Edward Island who would later become an Alberta senator. After a few weeks of digging, John wanted to get back to the cowboy life. He returned to the Bar U.

In the spring of 1884, John took a leading role in the first multi-ranch round-up. Six large cattle ranches had turned their herds loose to graze on their leased lands. Ranging freely, the cattle had intermingled with no regard for brands or ownership. A team effort was needed to round them up. Altogether the round-up organizers brought in 100 cowboys, 500 horses, and 15 chuckwagons.

John and the Bar U crew of

Tom Graham, an 18-year-old cowboy, 1893. Many young cowboys had to prove their worth during round-ups.

about 20 cowboys rode to Fort Macleod, where they met up with outfits from the other ranches. The cowboys split into two large parties, one heading west and the other east. The Bar U crew joined the party heading east and rode southeast as far as the border south of Lethbridge. Then the round-up routine got underway.

Breakfast was at 4:30—often just cups of thick coffee. Then the cowboys set out to round up cattle and drive them back to graze near their camp. After a brief break for lunch, they went out to round up more cattle. Supper was at five or six, and then some cowboys returned to the range for night duty.

The rounded-up cattle were grouped in herds of about a thousand head. Each herd had to be contained day and night by riders working in pairs. They circled the herd in opposite directions until they were relieved by the next shift. The calves were cut out of the herd and branded. Then each ranch outfit moved its stock to a watering hole where some of its cowboys were camped. When one ranch's herd was completely rounded up, the cowboys drove the cattle to their home range. John and the Bar U crew rode the dusty trail for two months. In all, the cowboys from the six ranches rounded up over 60,000 head of cattle.

When the round-up was over, John took another short break from cowboy life. Gold fever had struck again. The previous summer when John and Dan Riley were digging at the Highwood River crossing, they heard wild tales about Lost Lemon Mine. In 1870 two Americans named Lemon and Blackjack were prospecting for gold in the Livingstone Mountains southwest of the Highwood River. They found huge nuggets in a stream and then struck the motherlode above a rocky ledge. Soon after, they quarrelled. In a moment of rage, Lemon killed his partner. Lemon panicked, fled their camp, and became lost in the hills. Nearly starved and mostly mad, he eventually reached Montana. A party of gold hunters set out with Lemon to find the mine, but he could not retrace his steps.

At Highwood River, John and Dan Riley had met Lafayette French, who told them he knew where the mine was located. So, in the summer of 1884, the pair hooked up with French and set out to find gold. They travelled on foot up stream beds leading into the Livingstone Mountains. They hiked, told stories, and looked for gold. Before long John realized that that this was a fool's expedition. Once again he decided to return to the cowboy

In 1884, just before the first big round-up, George Lane was hired as the new Bar U foreman. The year before, he had driven 1,800 head of cattle from Montana to the Belly River range in Alberta District. When the Bar U expanded, his managerial skills made it one of the most successful ranches in Alberta. Lane was known for his keen knowledge of ranching—and his toughness.

life. This time he took a job at the Quorn Ranch, located north of the Bar U.

In May 1885 John took part in the second multi-ranch spring round-up. It was even bigger than the round-up of 1884, with hundreds of cowboys and more than a thousand saddle horses. George Lane, the new foreman at the Bar U, was in charge of the round-up, but John's unflagging stamina and expert skills with cows and horses made him a key figure. He saved the life of a cowboy who had been thrown from his horse with one foot caught in a stirrup. Remembering his own days as a greenhorn, John went out of his way to help the round-up's rookies. There was no school for cowboys, but John was a natural teacher, generous with both his time and his advice.

There was no way John could have known that this spring round-up was a milestone. It was the last one to make a single sweep through the whole open range from the Alberta-Montana border to the outskirts of Calgary. Afterwards neighbouring ranches organized regional round-ups. By 1885 there were too many cattle on the range—almost 100,000—to sort out in a single round-up. This round-up was special for another reason. It took place as the threat of war hung over cowboy country.

When the North-West Rebellion broke out in the Saskatchewan District of the North-West Territories in 1885, fear spread like wild fire through the District of Alberta. Soon John Ware would be taking on another responsibility— patrolling the range as a volunteer scout.

Unrest had been building among Saskatchewan's Métis and Native people for more than a year. The Métis were losing their land and their way of life to new settlers arriving on the CPR, and the Canadian government was failing the Native people. It had cut meat rations on the reserves and people were starving. Once again the Métis turned to Louis Riel, who had led them in the Red River Rebellion in 1870. In March 1885 Riel proclaimed a provisional government in the Saskatchewan

District. In the next few months protest turned to violence as the Métis and Cree clashed with the North-West Mounted Police and government troops.

The First Nations living on reserves in Alberta had the same grievances as the Cree in Saskatchewan. Would the Blackfoot, Stoney, Sarcee, and Piegan also rebel against the government? Emergency meetings were held in Calgary and in smaller towns to discuss what to do. The Canadian government appointed Thomas Strange, a local rancher and retired major-general, to head the Alberta Field Force. In April volunteers streamed into Calgary to join up. Superintendent Sam Steele of the North-West Mounted Police was put in charge of the Force's scouts, who were mainly cowboys, young men from the Stoney Nation, and members of the NWMP. Steele's Scouts accompanied the Alberta Field Force as it marched out of Calgary.

When the Alberta Field Force left town, Calgarians felt defenceless. Entirely false rumours were creating panic: Native people on nearby reserves were on the march, cutting telegraph lines and tearing up the CPR. The mayor and elected officials seemed paralyzed, so a retired NWMP officer, James Walker, organized the Home Guard to protect the town.

Fear was also racing through cattle country. Eleven-year-old Julia Short wrote in her diary about precautions taken at High River:

Government troops at Fish Creek. When the Métis defeated the NWMP at Duck Lake, the Canadian government responded quickly. It sent troops from eastern Canada on the nearly completed railway. The Métis and Cree were out-numbered and out-armed. After a few pitched battles, the rebels were defeated. Their leader, Louis Riel, was captured at Batoche and later hanged for treason.

Sam Steele was a legend in the West. In 1870 he had been part of the military force that put down the Riel Rebellion in Manitoba. In 1873 he joined the NWMP and helped establish police posts across the North-West Territories. Among railway workers, cowboys, settlers, and First Nations, Sam Steele was respected as a tough and fearless, but fair, policeman.

Crowfoot, Father Lacombe, and Three Bulls. Missionaries and First Nations chiefs helped keep the District of Alberta peaceful in 1885.

April 10, 1885: Ten men volunteered to fight between here and Medicine Hat and they formed a Home Guard but they have to be sworn in yet. Charlie [her brother] is one of the Home Guard. They take turns watching out on the ridge for signs of Indians coming and have material to light a warning fire. We girls are supposed to stay close to home but we have a place in the woods picked out to hide in case of emergency. Each night the horses are left with harness on, except the bridles, and the wagon hauled up close to the house, our telescope bags packed with valuables and necessities in case we have to start for Calgary in a hurry.

The Home Guard was protecting people in towns, but what about the ranchers on the open range? They would have to take care of themselves. Volunteers from ranches near the foothills formed the Rocky Mountain Rangers, led by Kootenai Brown. They patrolled the area between Fort Macleod and Medicine Hat.

John Ware joined another unit of volunteer scouts, organized by Bar U manager Fred Stimson. Stimson's Scouts patrolled the open range around High River and into the Porcupine Hills. John and the other rangers rode in pairs, keeping their eyes open for trouble as they checked their cattle. The Native people on the reserves were hungry, and the temptation to steal stray cattle was hard to resist. Several times John and his partner confronted young Native men roaming the open range. They were armed and sometimes out-numbered the scouts. In each confrontation John argued for peace, and the young men listened. Among the First Nations, John was respected for his strength and honesty. His calm but imposing presence convinced potential young rebels to put down their arms and return to their reserves.

John didn't see any military action during the rebellion.

Cowboys in the District of Alberta

In 1883 a Calgary newspaper writer declared that cowboys were "the best fellows in the world, good hearted and generous and always ready to assist a man in trouble." Not all cowboys who rode the Alberta range were as "good hearted and generous" as John Ware, but John liked most of the cowboys he met.

The cowboys in early Alberta came from all over the world and from many different backgrounds. They made their way from Ontario, Quebec, Britain, Ireland, Scotland, France, Norway, Mexico, and the United States. Many arrived as greenhorns looking for adventure. Others brought years of experience and well-honed skills. Some of the best cowboys were the

Métis cowboys Alex Gladstone and Dan Nault, from Pincher Creek, posing in a studio portrait, 1900.

expert horsemen who had grown up on the plains of Alberta hunting buffalo—men like Joe Red Blanket and Daniel Little Axe from the Blackfoot Nation and Bobtail Chief and Heavy Head from the Blood Nation. Also among the best were Métis cowboys from Wood Mountain, Pincher Creek, and Maple Creek.

John Ware was not the only Black cowboy in

the District of Alberta. Green Walters arrived from the American West in 1883 just as John had done a year earlier—on a cattle drive led by Tom Lynch. John probably crossed trails with a few other Black cowboys, such as Tom Rengald from the Chipman Ranch, Felix Luttrell from the Little Bow Ranch, and Jim Whitford from the Hyssop Ranch.

Nor did he really expect to. He knew that both Crowfoot, chief of the Blackfoot Nation, and Red Crow, leader of the Blood Nation, wanted to maintain good relations—despite their grievances and the unrest among their young men. In the end, the people of the District of Alberta escaped war, thanks to peacemakers like Chief Crowfoot and John Ware.

Just three years after he arrived in the District of Alberta, John Ware was making a name for himself. In June 1885 a writer for the *Macleod Gazette* declared: "John is not only one of the best natured and most obliging fellows in the country, but he is one of the shrewdest cowmen, and the man is considered pretty lucky who has him to look after his interest. The horse is not running on the prairie which John cannot ride sitting with his face either to the head or the tail, and even if the animal chooses to stand on its head or lie on its back, John always appears on top when the horse gets up, and smiles as if he enjoyed it—and he probably does." Even among such a rugged group as Alberta's early cowboys, John Ware stood out.

Chapter 3
Keeping Company with Cattle Barons

I t was September 1885. The spring round-up was over, and Stimson's Scouts had disbanded. John Ware was restless. He decided to sign on to a cattle drive heading for the stockyards in Calgary.

John hoped that this trip to Calgary would be better than his last one. A year earlier John had arrived in the town just after a Black man had been accused of murder. The townspeople were stirred up, and the sight of another Black man on their streets fired their racism. They made it very clear that John was not welcome in their town. John was known for his calm nature, but one thing could fire his temper: racists who judged him by his skin colour rather than his character. Would he get a better reception in Calgary this time?

As the herd approached Calgary on the Macleod Trail, John noted two worn trails leading to the Elbow River. One led to a whisky-trading post and the other to a Roman

Calgary as it looked when John Ware rode into town in 1885.

This cowboy has donned full cowboy dress for a studio photograph, sometime in the 1880s.

Catholic mission, both built in the 1870s. As the herd crossed the Elbow River bridge into town, John could see that Calgary was growing. When the Canadian Pacific Railway reached the town in 1883, it had started an economic boom that was in full swing. From a little settlement, Calgary had developed into a market town for the surrounding cattle country. Dealers eagerly bought up cattle. A growing number of merchants sold supplies to the cowboys and ranchers from nearby spreads. By 1885 the population had shot up to about 500 people.

As John rode into the main part of town, he could see I.G. Baker's general store on his right. Behind it he saw the flagpole of Fort Calgary. John and the crew turned the herd towards the stockyards near the CPR station on Centre Street. After the herd was delivered, John looked around the busy streets. From horseback he could see the Calgary Town Hall that had been finished the year before. He saw new stores and blacksmith shops, a bath house, a barber shop, even a photographic studio.

On the streets John recognized cowboys he had met on round-ups. They were easy to pick out in their worn clothes and battered hats and by the tough cayuses they had tied to hitching posts. Some were still dusting themselves off after riding into town. Others were leaning unsteadily on the horse rails outside the hotels. John nodded to them, then shook his head in wonder at another group of cowboys. They were lounging outside a saddle shop dressed in fancy chaps, spurs as big as saucers, and sombreros.

John moved on past these young peacocks and dismounted at the I.G. Baker store. He had heard that Baker's was looking for someone to work behind the counter. When John inquired about the job, he got a cold stare. But he was offered a job unloading freight wagons behind the store where customers couldn't see him. John sensed that there was racism behind the offer, but he took the job. He needed the money to fulfill a dream.

John felt a distinct coolness whenever he met townspeople on the streets. One day the North-West Mounted Police questioned him about some missing horses. He thought he had been treated as a suspect just because he was a Black man. John had had enough of Calgary. He decided to go back to the open range where, as the cowboy saying went, "A good man or a good horse is never a bad colour."

As he thought about returning to cattle country, John's mind was focused on a big dream—buying a ranch of his own. He had already taken the first steps. He'd been working hard and saving money. In May he had registered his own cattle brand, now officially listed in the ledger book: "9999 on left rib registered to John Ware, May 25 1885."

John thought about his next step. He needed more money in his pocket to look for land to buy. In his last job at the Quorn Ranch, he had worked with the ranch's large stable of horses. And John liked horses more than cattle. So he decided to return to the Quorn.

John was put in charge of the horses at the Quorn Ranch. He broke broncs and trained cayuses. And for the first time he was working with expensive, purebred horses imported from Britain. There were magnificent thoroughbred stallions, the foundation of the Quorn's horse-breeding program. The Quorn owners had also sent over Cleveland Bays, a breed of hunters and jumpers. Neither John nor most of the people in Alberta had ever seen such elegant animals. With John in charge, the Quorn soon gained an excellent reputation for breeding quality horses. They commanded high prices and stud fees throughout the North-West Territories.

One day John's old trail boss, Tom Lynch, stopped at the Quorn Ranch to ask for advice. Lynch was delivering a string of horses to Montana. As payment, he could choose one of the mares to keep. Without hesitation, John picked out his favourite. That mare became the mother of May W, a very successful racehorse. (May W was shipped to England for breeding, but some of her descendants returned to Canada and were still racing in the 1950s.) John Ware clearly had a good eye for horses.

Cattle Barons and Ranch Companies

*I*n 1885 big ranch companies owned by wealthy cattle barons were flourishing in the District of Alberta. The leasing system introduced by the Canadian government in 1881 and the building of the CPR had created a cattle boom. Seventy-five leases were granted in 1882 and about 20 more in the next two years. By 1886, 8.5 million acres (about 3.4 million hectares) had been leased.

Setting up a large cattle operation required a big budget and wealthy investors. The investors were cattle barons, some of whom enjoyed their profits without setting foot on a ranch. They invested their profits in Calgary's real estate boom and in other Alberta industries, such as meat-packing plants, brickworks, sawmills, and power companies. The day-to-day running of the ranches was left to managers. They tended to be well-educated men with business experience and good connections to influential people.

For just a handful of men, the ranch company owners and their managers wielded a lot of power in the District of Alberta. They helped set up stockbreeders' associations and the first school boards. They sat on the board of directors of Calgary's first hospital and became involved in local politics. A few sat in the legislature for the North-West Territories.

Brickworks at the Cochrane Ranche, about 1900.

In John Ware's day, five big companies dominated the cattle business in the District of Alberta. John had spent his first years working at the most successful one—the North-West Cattle Company at the Bar U Ranch. The North-West Cattle Company's major rival was the Cochrane Ranche Company. Its founder, Matthew H. Cochrane, leased 100,000 acres (40,400 hectares) on the Bow River at the Big Hill range west of Calgary and bought 17,000 head of American cattle. Many of them died on the open range in the hard winters of 1881 and 1882. In 1883 Cochrane moved the main herd to the more sheltered Waterton area. By 1885 Cochrane held leases on about 335,000 acres (135,000 hectares) of grazing land.

The Oxley Ranche Company was based on the Willow Creek range between the Bar U Ranch and Fort Macleod. A wealthy Ontario cattle breeder, John R. Craig, took out the origi-nal lease and found investors in England: Member of Parliament Alexander Staveley Hill and the Earl of Lathom. Hill was managing director and Craig was ranch manager. By the winter of 1883-84 the company held 200,000 acres (81,000 hectares) of land, about 3,000 cattle, and 300 horses.

Matthew H. Cochrane, a wealthy cattle breeder from Quebec and a strong supporter of the Conservative Party, was appointed to the Canadian Senate in 1872. Senator Cochrane saw the opportunity for huge profits in cattle ranching in the North-West Territories, and gave Prime Minister John A. Macdonald a set of recommendations that became the basis of the 1881 leasing system. As soon as the scheme was introduced, Cochrane established the Cochrane Ranche Company.

The Walrond Ranche Company was started by Dr. Duncan McEachran, who had been chief government veterinarian in Alberta. He recruited Sir John Walrond-Walrond, a prominent mem-ber of the British Conservative Party, as the main investor. As ranch manager, McEachran ran the day-to-day operations of the Walrond (or as John and other locals called it, "the Waldron").

The Quorn Ranch was started by an Englishman, C.W. Martin. He found investors among the gentry of the Quorn Hunt Club in Leicestershire. The Quorn owners leased land in the Fish Creek area, and then sent 90 head of prized Angus cattle to start their herd. When it was in full operation, the ranch grazed about 5,000 head of cattle. From the beginning, horse breeding was a central part of the Quorn operation. The ranch's directors saw Alberta as the perfect place to breed quality horses for fox hunting and as mounts for the British cavalry. At its height, the ranch had more than 1,200 horses. The manager was J.J. Barter, a stockman who was so well known and respected by local cowboys and ranchers that the trail between the Quorn Ranch and Calgary was called "the Barter Trail."

English fashion and English sports influenced life on some of Alberta's big ranches.

John's skill with horses made him a valuable asset at the Quorn. And his expertise and good nature made him a hit with the English gentry who visited the ranch. They were the relatives and friends of the Quorn's directors out visiting the colonies for a bit of adventure. John may have been a little reserved when he first met these well-educated and elegantly mannered men. Some of them were titled and all of them were wealthy. But he accepted them openly and spoke to them honestly.

For their part, some of the English visitors found it hard to step away from their prejudices. To them, a Black man in North America was either a servant or a menial worker. Yet John's confident manner and direct talk did not fit that image, and he quickly won their affection and respect. And there was no question that John had plenty to teach them.

Most of the visitors fancied they knew quite a lot about horses. They had been riding well-trained horses and hunting foxes across England's green countryside for most of their lives, and some owned their own stables. Yet they soon learned from John that riding a cayuse was a whole different matter.

John taught the Quorn visitors how to ride western style. He took them out on the open range and showed them how to keep their horses from stumbling into gopher holes. John also organized fox hunts at the Quorn, complete with hounds imported from England. John was responsible for the care and breeding of the hounds, as well as training them to chase coyotes— Alberta's equivalent of the British fox.

One day John was invited to join the gentry at a formal dinner at the Quorn Ranch. The English gentlemen were in full evening dress, and John could not help but stare at their finery. One man noticed John's interest and promised to ask his tailor make a dress suit for John. John wondered if this was an idle promise, but soon enough a package

arrived from England. Inside was a dress suit, including a long frock coat that John proudly wore for years.

A group of ranchers, with John Ware sitting in the centre of the front row. Some wear clothing influenced by British styles.

Sometimes John demonstrated feats of strength that amazed not only the gentry but also the Quorn's cowboys. One visitor challenged John to straighten a curved hay hook with his bare hands—and he did. On a bet, John lifted a barrel full of water and deposited it on a nearby cart. Then he lifted a wagon box off its frame.

The Quorn gentry enjoyed hearing stories about John Ware. One story took place in Calgary in 1887. George Lane of the Bar U asked J.J. Barter for John's help in driving a cattle herd to the CPR depot in Calgary. The herd bunched up as the cowboys tried to funnel them through a chute and into the rail cars. So tightly packed were the cattle that no one, including John, could ride into the jam. John dismounted, stood on the back of the nearest cow, and then walked across the backs of the cattle towards the chute—just like a lumberjack walking on logs floating in a river. He reached down and manhandled the animals out of the blocked entrance. The herd started moving through the chute again.

J.J. Barter's favourite story was about John's stamina and

determination. It was winter and John was treating a sick horse. He set out on horseback to buy turpentine and oil to make a liniment. John reached the store at Highwood Crossing, bought two big crocks of the ingredients he needed, and set out to return to the ranch. On the way a blizzard hit. His horse struggled against the wind and snow but found it impossible to move forward. John dismounted, slung the heavy crocks onto his own back, and led the exhausted horse through the dark night back to the Quorn Ranch.

Winter always took its toll in the District of Alberta—on cowboys, horses, and especially cattle. For the Quorn and other ranches on the Alberta range, the winter of 1886-1887 hit hard. Cattle died in droves. Some died where they stood on the open range. Others clustered together in coulees or at the foot of cliffs in a desperate attempt to find warmth from each other. At winter's end, cowboys found dead cattle stacked six deep in the coulees. Some of the animals had been so starved for food that they sucked the hair from the hides of the dead beasts and their throats were matted with it.

The Quorn owners in faraway England had never experienced an Alberta winter. They assumed that bad management explained the loss of so many cattle. This was one reason why the Quorn's manager, J.J. Barter, found himself increasingly at odds with the British owners. There was another reason. The owners would not abandon their plan for a big horse-breeding operation at the Quorn Ranch. They still intended to stock English hunt stables and British cavalry regiments with Alberta-bred horses. They overlooked the high overseas shipping costs and the depressingly low prices the ranch's horses were fetching in England.

Despite the trouble brewing at the Quorn, John continued working with the horses. Sometimes he was back on the range, checking the herd that was grazing on the ranch's lease or riding long distances to retrieve stray cattle or sell stock. On one trip into the Turner Valley, he rode with Sam Howe, a veteran American cowboy who had started a small ranch on Sheep Creek. Looking for water for their horses, they spotted a pond. As they approached, they noticed a strong smell and a dark scum on the water. The horses refused to drink, so John and Sam turned away. Out of curiosity John threw a burning match, and the pond burst into flame. Later John delivered a

sample of the substance floating on the water to a Calgary chemist and asked him to analyze it. According to the chemist, it was coal seepage that had no value or use. For John that was the end of the matter. It may be, however, that John and Sam were among the first to stumble on Alberta's rich oil resource.

Sometimes J.J. Barter sent John out to evict squatters who had settled on land that was part of the Quorn's grazing lease. Often the settlers refused to move. One pointed out that he was actually outside the Quorn boundary. Another told John that he knew the land was soon to be surveyed by the government and then it would be legally his.

His experience with these settlers made John think hard about the changes that were rolling across the District of Alberta. The Canadian Pacific Railway, which had reached Calgary in 1883, was bringing more settlers. And the government's land-leasing policy, which had once favoured cattle barons, was being replaced by a policy that favoured homesteaders. In 1888 the government stopped granting new leases for grazing land and cancelled leases held by absentee landlords. Except for leases held by the established ranches, the District of Alberta was wide open to homesteaders.

It was time for John to get his own spread before good land became scarce. He had a registered cattle brand. He had purchased a few unbranded and unclaimed cattle, called mavericks, from the High River Stockmen's Association. And he had his eye on a piece of land on Sheep Creek. His next step was to register the land under the Dominion Lands Act. The Canadian government had passed the act in 1872 to encourage settlement. It provided 160 acres (about 65 hectares) of free land

Settlers migrating into the Alberta District. The arrival of waves of settlers marked the end of open-range cattle ranching in Alberta.

A CPR train at the Calgary station, 1884. The completed CPR brought many new settlers to the West.

to each head of a family or 21-year-old male who paid the $10 registration fee. In return, these homesteaders had to live on the land for three years, cultivate 30 acres (about 12 hectares), and build a permanent residence.

In 1889—with his dream about to come true—John took a job at the High River Horse Ranch. It had been set up by English owners a couple of years before to breed horses for the army and the North-West Mounted Police. Once again John would be working with a fine stock of thoroughbreds and a kennel of hounds—this time as ranch foreman. His pay was $55 a month, a lot more than most cowboys made. There was another big advantage to the job at the High River Horse Ranch. It was located close to Sheep Creek. John could find the perfect site for his ranch, register a homestead grant, and begin to build a house—and his new life as an independent rancher.

Chapter 4
A Ranch at Sheep Creek

John chose a piece of land for his own ranch on the north shore of Sheep Creek. By 1890 he had built a house between the creek and a sheltering hill. His homestead was close to Millarville, where Malcolm Millar operated a store and trading post. When John moved into his house, there were already a few small ranches on Sheep Creek. His old friend Sam Howe was ranching nearby, and John soon set out to meet his other neighbours.

Sheep Creek valley where John decided to homestead.

John and Kate Quirk had settled on the north shore of Sheep Creek a few years earlier. They had left Ireland in the 1850s, settled in Detroit, Michigan, and then reached Alberta by way of Montana. John was a frequent visitor to their ranch, where he enjoyed swapping tales with the well-travelled Quirks. John Quirk told stories about his days at the gold camps in California. Kate told about their stay at Mosquito Creek near Fort Macleod, where the insects were so thick that Kate claimed she "scraped them off the tent and made soup."

A young Scot named Alexander Aird lived between John's ranch and the Quirk's. He had arrived in 1889 and was hoping to homestead as soon as the land was surveyed. Nearby on the same branch of Sheep Creek was Joseph Deane-Freeman and his family. He had arrived in 1887 with his wife, five children, a nursemaid, and a manservant. All of them had lived together in a tent until their house was built.

On the south shore of Sheep Creek, John met Walter and Agrippa (Grip) Vine from Dorset, England. The two brothers had worked their way through the United States and the North-West Territories building levees on the Mississippi, hauling freight in the Dakotas, and laying down rail beds for the CPR. They had registered their homestead claim in 1889. Now, like John, they were getting their start as ranchers.

John often ran into his neighbours on the Sheep Creek range. They were homesteading their own claims, but they still grazed their cattle on the surrounding land that had not been yet surveyed or homesteaded. Each winter the cattle belonging to the small ranchers intermingled with the big herds from the Quorn and the Bar U. Each spring John and his neighbours took part in the Sheep Creek round-up to reclaim their cows and calves and help sort out the others.

Whenever John's eyes wandered over the river valley and gentle hills around his new ranch, he felt a real sense of accomplishment. It had been a long, hard journey from slavery in South Carolina to operating his own ranch in the foothills of Alberta. But he was not completely content. John Ware wanted to share his life and good fortune with a wife and family.

Canadian emigration offices in the U.S., Britain, and the rest of Europe advertised free land in the West.

Finding a wife in the District of Alberta was no easy matter. There were few women in the ranching community, about one woman for every three men in the area around Calgary. For John, the chances of finding a wife were even more difficult. He had made it clear to his friends that he wanted to marry a Black woman, but there were only 27 Black settlers in the whole district. So John took special notice when J.J. Barter arrived with some news. His old boss at the Quorn told him that the Lewises, a Black family with a 19-year-old daughter, had settled on the

　　　A Ranch at Sheep Creek

outskirts of Calgary.

Daniel Lewis, his wife Charlotte, and their four children had taken up a homestead near Shepard, southeast of Calgary. Daniel had earned a living as a carpenter in Toronto. (Eventually his expert work would adorn the finest houses in Calgary.) The family boarded the Canadian Pacific Railway in Toronto and joined a host of other families migrating to the District of Alberta.

The Lewises were part of a wave of homesteaders who arrived in Alberta in the late 1880s and early 1890s. In 1889 Calgary had set up an immigration committee, and part of its job was distributing pamphlets to attract homesteaders from eastern Canada. By 1891 new settlers had pushed the non-Native population of Alberta to 17,500, up from 1,000 just ten years earlier. They were the forerunners of the great tide of immigrants that would transform Alberta at the turn of the twentieth century.

It wasn't long before John had devised a plan to meet the Lewises. He discovered that they shopped every Saturday in the I.G. Baker Company store in Calgary. John avoided Calgary as much as possible, but he began to visit the store on Saturdays. His scheme paid off. When the family came into the store one Saturday, John shyly introduced himself to Daniel and Charlotte Lewis—and to their daughter Mildred.

Mildred Lewis

The family invited John to dinner. He readily accepted the invitation, and the next one, and the next one. Even when he became a regular guest in their home, John was not really sure how pleased Mr. and Mrs. Lewis were that he was showing an interest in their daughter. After all, he was big and rugged—every inch a cowboy. And John knew that it was easy to get a poor impression of cowboys. Cowboys still roared into Calgary to spend their pay and let off steam. Occasionally brawls spilled out from hotels onto the streets. Sometimes impromptu horse races created clouds of dust in the centre of town.

John was full of doubts. Mildred and the rest of the Lewis family were well educated for the time. He was an expert in the ways of cows, horses, and hounds, but he couldn't read or write. The Lewises were also church-goers and they loved music—they had brought a piano with them all the way from Ontario. And then there was the issue of age. John was 26 years older than Mildred. Would her parents think he was too old for their daughter? And John had noticed something else. Mildred herself seemed unsure about how to respond to her cowboy suitor.

John was invited to spend the Christmas of 1891 with the Lewis family. His gift to Mildred was very special—a silver brooch he had purchased in Calgary. Perhaps it was a sign that their courtship was over and their engagement had begun. For John, former slave and cowboy, another dream was coming true.

On February 29, 1892, John and Mildred were married in Calgary. *The Calgary Tribune* carried their wedding announcement: "Very many of our readers will join with us in wishing Mr. John Ware and bride, who were married Tuesday morning, all happiness and prosperity in their new sphere of life. The ceremony was performed by the Rev. Mr. Cross, pastor of the Baptist Church, at the residence of the bride's parents in Calgary. The bride is of a happy disposition, well cultured and accomplished, and probably no man in the district has a greater number of warm personal friends than the groom, Mr. John Ware."

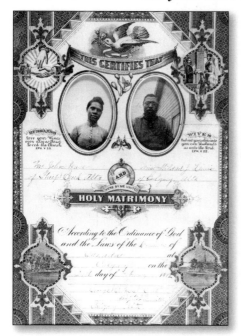

John and Mildred Ware's marriage certificate.

Before his wedding John had built a new home for his bride. It was a sturdy frame house made of sawn lumber. There was a comfortable sitting room and two bedrooms in the main part of the house. In the attached lean-to was a kitchen and a small bedroom for a ranch hand.

Suddenly Mildred found herself living on an isolated ranch. She had grown up in Toronto surrounded by neighbours, and even the Lewis homestead, which was on a main trail close to Calgary, had a few neighbours close by. John's neighbours at Sheep Creek were not even within sight of the ranch. Some of the surrounding land had not yet been surveyed, and not all of the surveyed sections had been homesteaded. At her new home, Mildred faced open range as far as the eye could see.

The Ware ranch house at Sheep Creek, 1896. The neat yard, fence, and corral show that the Ware ranch was well-established after just six years.

Mildred knew little about horses, cattle, and ranch life. But like many other pioneer women in Alberta, she was soon up to her ears in daily chores. She milked cows, churned butter, and tended a large garden. She made clothes and did carpentry jobs in the new house. Her husband, who was better at handling a herd than a hammer, was happy to see that his new wife had inherited her father's skills.

Not long after the ranch house was completed, it echoed with the cries of their first child. Janet (Nettie) Ware was born in 1893. Robert was born the following year. Twins William and Mildred Jane arrived in 1898, and Arthur in 1900. Except for Nettie, who was born in Calgary, all the children were born at home with the help of a neighbour's wife. John and Mildred considered themselves lucky. All the children born at Sheep Creek survived infancy. Infant deaths were common in pioneer families, especially those who lived in isolated areas where there was no doctor closer than a day's ride. Not long after she arrived at Sheep Creek, Mildred had helped John bury the infant daughter of his friend Sam Howe.

The Sheep Creek ranch was isolated, but the Wares had their share of visitors. Sam Howe turned up and so did John and Kate Quirk, Alexander Aird, and Walter and Agrippa Vine. Other visitors included the Fiddlers, a Métis family, and neighbours who had immigrated from Mexico. Men from the nearby

A Sarcee camp. John and Mildred always welcomed Sarcee visitors at their Sheep Creek ranch.

Sarcee reserve were drawn to the Ware ranch by John's reputation for neighbourliness and his ability to speak to them in their own language. Sometimes they stopped by when they were out looking for cattle that had strayed from the reserve. Other times they were hungry and Mildred fed them.

When Mildred and John needed a few supplies, they went to Millarville. A post office had been added to the Millars' store, so the Wares would shop, send their mail, and visit with Malcolm and Helen Millar. When they stayed for tea, they might sit down with a dozen or more of their far-flung neighbours. Usually John also stopped in to see Constable Oaks of the North-West Mounted Police. Oaks patrolled the great stretch of range from Calgary to High River, and John was always interested in his news about local ranchers—and rustlers. Like most ranchers in the area, John had lost some cattle to rustlers. In November 1893 the *Calgary Herald* offered a $500 reward for information leading to a conviction against rustlers caught handling cattle with certain brands. John's brand was one of those listed.

Somehow in the midst of the hard work of ranching, the Wares and their neighbours found time for dances. Usually they were organized in the winter, when the cattle were on the range and there were fewer chores. Families thought nothing of driving 30 kilometres by sleigh to a dance. They wrapped themselves in blankets and used heated rocks to warm their feet. Single cowboys rode to the dances carrying their best clothes in burlap sacks slung over their saddles. When they reached the dance, they changed into their finest duds. John outfitted himself in his Prince Albert coat. Everyone was on the floor as soon as the musicians brought out their fiddles and mouth organs, and they danced through most of the night.

No one set out for home until the morning. It was too dangerous travelling at night in the winter. One of the Wares' neighbours had learned that lesson the hard way. She had been returning home from town with her baby when darkness fell. A light snow quickly turned into a blizzard. Less than a kilometre from home, she released the horses from the buggy and set out on foot, carrying the baby in her arms. Trying to feel her way through the blinding snow, she took one step at a time. Suddenly she plunged into water. It was the creek that passed by her farm, and she was able to follow it to the corral fence that led to the ranch house. Not everyone was as lucky.

John had purchased nine maverick cattle in 1888. By the time he and Mildred were married four years later, his herd had grown to more than 200 head. From his cowboy days on the open range, he had learned some hard lessons about raising cattle. He especially knew the mistakes he had to avoid.

He still remembered the terrible winter of 1886-87 when the Quorn and other ranches had lost so many cattle on the open range. He remembered, too, that ranchers who had hay to feed their cattle had suffered far fewer losses. One of John's top priorities was to grow and harvest enough hay to keep his cattle from starving during hard winters.

John decided that first he needed to irrigate his land to make a lush hay meadow. He had helped the Quirks dig an irrigation ditch from Sheep Creek onto their land. Now he

After devastating cattle losses over harsh winters, ranchers began to grow hay for winter feed.

did the same on his own land with the help of Joe Standish, a young man he had hired as his ranch hand. That fall John and Joe cut and stacked 200 tons (about 180 tonnes) of hay.

John needed more land to plant a crop of wheat, so he rented a meadow south of Sheep Creek from the Hudson's Bay Company. He also built a small cabin for Joe Standish, who would spend the winter tending the herd.

Mildred, Bob, Nettie, and John, about 1896.

John wanted to make sure that he could feed his growing family. Joe ploughed some land around the ranch house, and John extended the ditch from Sheep Creek to irrigate his fields of grain and vegetables. He also ran the ditch under a shed near the house where it kept milk, butter, and other perishables cool during hot weather.

The cool, dark shed with the ditch running through it was a magnet for the Ware children, especially in hot weather. Their father warned them against playing there. One day John discovered Bob playing above the fast-moving water. He quickly snatched up his son and dunked him in the stream. All of the children learned an important lesson that day.

John and Mildred were gentle, caring parents. Despite the hardships and isolation of ranch life, their children were happy. And John loved to join in their childish fun whenever he could. They played tag and chased each other and their dogs through the open fields. They explored the edges of the creek. They gathered wildflowers and collected insects. Of all the children, Nettie was the most curious. One cold winter day she wondered what would happen if she put her tongue on an iron anvil that had been sitting outdoors in frigid weather. She found out—it stuck!

And then there were chores to do. John taught all of his children to ride at an early age, and as they grew older, they mounted up to help their father tend the cattle. The younger children helped Mildred look after the chickens and weed the garden.

John's careful attention to his animals and his skill in selecting good stock eventually paid off. Between 1892 and 1898, he doubled the size of his herd. John was now in his fifties with a large family. He began again to dream about the future—about the days when his children would be running the ranch. In 1899 he asked Mildred to register cattle brands for their eldest children, Nettie and Bob.

John still rode the range in the Sheep Creek district checking his own herd and watching for strays that belonged to other ranchers. He always kept an eye out for wolves, which preyed on injured cattle and newborn calves. John had always been a skilled wolf hunter. In 1900 he organized a few cowboys who worked for the Quirks to help him hunt a pack of wolves that had been terrorizing cattle. They came across four wolves, and set their sights on one that was particularly huge and menacing. John yelled to shoot. One shot rang out, and the wolf fell. The three Quirk cowboys, young men who fancied they were pretty good shots, weren't fast enough. It was John who killed the wolf.

John's many talents were always welcome on the range and at neighbouring ranches. He organized and acted as captain of the spring round-up on the Sheep Creek range. He helped his neighbours and other ranchers drive their cattle to market and break wild broncs.

For a short time, John took a job at Fort Macleod breaking horses for the North-West Mounted Police. A police inspector from Regina turned up one day and tried to mount one of the horses. When he was promptly thrown, he accused John of failing to do his job properly. John responded quickly. He mounted the horse and held it firmly in check. Then he trotted around the fort's parade grounds and had the horse perform a

NWMP review, Fort Macleod, 1894. The NWMP needed well-disciplined horses and sometimes asked John Ware to train them.

few intricate turns. Finally he halted, dismounted, and walked away—leaving the horse standing obediently. It was an exhibition of such skilful horsemanship that even the indignant inspector was full of praise.

But it wasn't all work and no play. John and his old pals from the Quorn Ranch occasionally collected their hounds and rode to the hunt—Alberta-style—chasing coyotes across the prairie. There were horse races, bronc-riding contests, and other friendly matches between John and other cowboys who needed to let off steam after working hard on the range. They enjoyed throwing out challenges, competing against each other, and showing off their cowboy skills. It was the fun part of being a cowboy.

Organized competitions for cowboys, with formal rules and prizes, were becoming popular in the United States. And soon they made their way into Alberta. In 1891 a cowboy sports day was organized at Fort Macleod. It was a modest affair with just two cowboys competing in two events—calf roping and bronc riding. Two years later George Lane of the Bar U Ranch organized a steer-roping competition at the Calgary Midsummer Fair. A Calgary company sponsored two valuable prizes: a saddle worth a hundred dollars for the winner and silver-trimmed spurs and a bridle for the runner-up. John Ware was about to win the first Calgary rodeo event—in record time.

The *Calgary Tribune* reported the day's events. Following its coverage of the bicycle races, foot races, and horse races, it turned to the steer-roping contest:

> The great event of the day, the cowboy roping contest, was next called, and the crowd awaited with breathless interest a spectacle so novel and so exciting. There were three entries only, but they were all old cattlemen, who thoroughly understood the handling of a lariat. George Lane, of High River, first took the field, and a wild and vicious steer was turned out of the corral. At the first throw Mr. Lane caught the brute's horn, but it unfortunately broke, and the animal had to be recaptured. It then took some time to throw, but this was finally done in good style, and the steer satisfactorily tied up. Time, 4.55 [minutes]. John Weir [Ware] was the next competitor, and he was much more fortunate than Lane in catching his animal, in fact from the time that the steer was first caught till he was securely tied

up was so short that the spectators were hardly aware that it had been done. The time was 51 seconds, the best on record by 2 seconds. Mr. Todd, the third entry, made good speed, tying his steer up in 2.51 [minutes].

In 1894 a bronc-riding competition was added to the Calgary Midsummer Fair's cowboy program. To make things more interesting, the cowboy sports were billed as a friendly grudge match between Fort Macleod and High River cowboys. John Ware was on the High River team and heavily favoured to win the steer-roping event again. When his turn came, everything looked good—at first. He roped his steer in no time. But the rope slipped and the steer broke free. The crowd seemed more disappointed than John himself.

Ranchers, stock associations, and organizers of agricultural fairs and exhibitions started organizing more cowboy contests across Alberta. In 1900 Calgary hosted an international cowboy competition. A group of Montana cowboys arrived with a string of broncs and money to wager. They bet that the Canadian cowboys couldn't ride their broncs. But they did and won the stakes. Everywhere in the Canadian West, cowboy competitions got bigger, better organized, and attracted larger crowds, which sometimes included aristocrats, prime ministers, and royalty. Gradually people began adopting the American term for cowboy competitions— rodeos.

Steer-roping competition at the first Territorial Exposition, Regina, 1895.

When John Ware won his first steer-roping contest in Calgary in 1893, little did he know that he was contributing to the birth—19 years later—of the Calgary Stampede, the world's greatest rodeo.

Chapter 5
Changing Times

In 1900, as the new century began, John Ware was feeling uneasy. When he rode the trails to High River and Calgary, he saw more and more homesteaders breaking soil that had never been ploughed and planting crops. He saw new fences chopping up the open range, new railway lines cutting off cattle from their grass, and new settlements growing at old river crossings. It was clear to John that the days of open-range ranching were numbered.

The heyday of the cattle barons and their big ranch companies had already come to an end. John had left the Quorn Ranch at the right time. It had slowly declined through the 1890s, with the directors still trying to run the ranch like an English country estate. By 1900 all its stock had been sold. Within a few years the Cochrane Ranche closed its Bow River operation and the Oxley sold out. The manager of the much smaller Walrond spent most of his time trying to evict squatters. Only the Bar U continued to operate as a large cattle company, mostly because of Fred Stimson's skills as a manager.

Homesteaders arriving in the District of Alberta.

New settlers were winning the battle for land in the District of Alberta. They had organized the Alberta Settlers' Rights Association in Calgary in 1885. Since then, the group had been demanding that the Canadian government open up the ranch company leases. Tensions between settlers and ranchers spread across the District. Settlers burned off grassland leased by the ranchers and squatted near

water holes used by their grazing herds. Workers for the ranch companies pulled down squatters' cabins, tore out their fences, and turned cattle loose on settlers' crops. The friction was heightened by a newspaper war. The *Macleod Gazette* championed the settlers and the *Calgary Herald* backed the ranch companies.

The government's revisions to the leasing regulations in the late 1880s eased tensions somewhat. But it was the federal election in 1896 that finally sealed the fate of the cattle barons and their ranching companies. Senator Matthew Cochrane's son ran for the Conservatives in the District of Alberta and was defeated by the Liberal candidate, who had the support of the settlers. John A. Macdonald and his Conservative Party lost the election, and the Liberals under Wilfrid Laurier took power. Laurier's Minister of the Interior, Clifford Sifton, made western immigration his top priority. Thousands of posters and pamphlets in dozens of languages advertised the attractions of "The Last Best West" and "Land for the Millions." The result was a flood of immigrants.

Wilfrid Laurier, elected prime minister in 1896, promoted a policy of immigration to the West.

In 1900 almost 7,500 homestead claims were filed in the District of Alberta. By 1901 the population had risen to over 73,000. As the population soared, cattle leases fell. Changes to the leasing regulations reduced ranch company leases from over eight million acres (over three million hectares) in 1886 to half that number by 1888. By 1900 the figure had fallen to 610,000 acres (244,000 hectares).

John was uneasy about the new style of raising cattle that he was seeing around him. Feeding them grain and raising them in fenced fields just didn't feel right. If he couldn't carry on raising his cattle on the open range at Sheep Creek, maybe it was time to move.

The ever-growing lines of fences had not yet reached his Sheep Creek ranch, but John was not going to wait for that to happen. In 1900 the family decided to move to the Red Deer River area. John was worried not only about advancing settlement, but also about drought. The 1890s had been dry years, and grass in the area south of Calgary was withering. John had heard about the natural grasses near the Red Deer River. They were shorter, more nutritious, and drought-resistant. And the area still had plenty of open range, at least for now.

John had no trouble selling his Sheep Creek ranch. He purchased a quarter section of 160 acres (about 65 hectares) on the Red Deer River for $1,000. The new ranch was in the Duchess district near the whistle-stop town of Bantry, about 40 kilometres north of Brooks. John selected his best 300 cows, sold the rest, and hired a crew to drive his cattle to their new home. The first thing was to get the herd across the Bow River—and that meant going through Calgary.

On the day John drove his herd through Calgary—now a bustling town of almost 4,000—its citizens were startled out of their beds. The sound of cattle rattling over the old Bow Marsh Bridge echoed through the streets. Residents knew that town officials had outlawed cattle drives through town, yet there was no mistaking the sound of cattle moving over the wooden bridge.

John and his crew had pushed the cattle up the Macleod Trail into Calgary, then across the bridge spanning the Elbow River. Only after the herd had crossed the Elbow did the police inform John that cattle were prohibited from crossing Calgary's bridges. John was stumped. The chief of police told him that his cattle would have to swim across the Bow River. But the Bow was flooded, and John feared for his cattle's safety. Turning back wasn't an option. That would mean crossing the bridge over the Elbow River again and, according to the police, doing that was illegal.

Frustrated and suspicious that racism was at play, John made his decision. He would drive his cattle over the bridge and leave Calgary behind for good. John and his trail crew rose early the next morning. Before anyone else stirred, they drove the herd across the rickety bridge. It swayed, groaned, creaked, and cracked. Then the lead steer was across and the rest followed. Soon the herd was on the trail heading towards the family's new home on the Red Deer River.

While John helped drive the herd, Mildred and the children lurched along in the wagon filled with everything they owned. The trail was rough. In places it had deep ruts left behind by Red River carts. As the wagon moved slowly along, the family passed a "stopping place" beside the trail. Here travellers could get a meal of flapjacks, boiled beans, and sowbelly for 50 cents. They could also pay for overnight accommodation in a wooden bunk.

The Wares didn't stop. They preferred to cook their own meals and make camp off the trail. Later Nettie Ware, who was seven years old at the time, remembered picking delicious "bullberries" at one spot where the family set up camp.

Finally, after a week on the trail, the Wares arrived at the new ranch. Mildred must have been taken aback when she saw it. At Sheep Creek she had left behind a green, lush valley along a wooded river in gently rolling countryside. The new ranch was treeless and it bordered on dry badlands. Stunted grass grew on low rises and in shallow gullies. But John looked around with satisfaction. He knew the grass would withstand drought, and there were no fences in sight. He turned his herd loose on the open range. Then he began to look for a site to build the family's new ranch house.

As he thought about the best site for the new house, John reminded himself that the weather had been very dry in recent years. He was thinking about digging another irrigation ditch, so building close to the banks of the Red Deer River seemed to make sense. John and his cattle crew quickly built a log house. It had a dirt floor and a sod roof, but it was home.

In the spring of 1902, disaster hit. The family woke up in the middle of the night to the sight and sound of water flooding the house. John hurried everyone to high ground and then returned to rescue what he could. As he carried their possessions to safety, he noticed a piece of paper floating in the water. It was his and Mildred's marriage certificate.

To rebuild the family's home after a flood, John used logs that he retrieved from the Red Deer River.

The flood took away their home, but it also provided materials for a new one. The raging Red Deer River had washed out a sawmill farther up the river. John spent several days salvaging logs with his lariat and hauling them to shore.

John and Mildred decided to build their new house back from the river well above the flood plain. They picked a site near a coulee and a small creek. As he began to clear the site, John's old friend Sam Howe appeared. He

The Ware family's new ranch house near the Red Deer River.

had just returned from the Boer War in South Africa. Howe joked that he had survived the war only because he had ridden a horse that John had bred. Sam helped John and Mildred build the new house. Although this one was also made of logs, it was much bigger than the first. It had a large main section and a smaller rear wing connected by a hallway. With a new roof over their heads, the Wares settled into ranch life again.

Once or twice a year the family took a shopping trip into Calgary. Later Nettie remembered returning home with mounds of dried fruit, flour, sugar, and beans piled in the wagon. Nettie also remembered fishing and picking Saskatoon berries, chokecherries, and buffalo berries to help feed the family. John hunted prairie chickens, ducks, geese, deer, and antelope. One particular antelope stood out in the children's mind. While their parents were away, a hired hand saw an antelope through the window and reached for a rifle hanging on the wall. The Ware children were standing on a bed to get a good view. The gun discharged and the bullet whizzed past them, embedding itself in the wall.

Life on the new ranch was not easy. John was often away looking after the cattle and taking part in round-ups. Mildred and the children were left in charge of the ranch and the chores. John was putting most of their money into building up his stock of cattle and horses, so Mildred had to use all her skill and ingenuity to meet the family's needs. She made all their clothes, sometimes from flour sacks. She grew and preserved vegetables and local berries.

Since there was no school nearby, Mildred was also in charge of the children's early education. She taught them at home until they were old enough to attend school in Blairmore, where they lived with Mildred's parents. John and Mildred missed their children when they went off to school. For a man who loved his children, sending them so far away to school must have been one of John's most difficult times. But for a man who could neither read nor write, it must also have been one of his proudest moments.

Chapter 6
Triumph and Tragedy

The first years in their new home were hard but satisfying for John and Mildred. In 1903 *The Farmers Advocate* newspaper wrote these words about the Wares:

> *Happiness and prosperity has been the lot of John and his wife. Five children are growing up to appreciate the value of Canadian freedom and Canadian justice; while John, as he views his herd of 650 cattle and 50 horses, his home and his happy wife and family, marvels at the greatness of a country that will enable a man who was born as a slave, and started life with a slave's disadvantages, to call so much of this world's goods his own and enjoy a measure of freedom and justice such as can be had in scarcely any other country in the world.*

Mildred with William, Arthur, and Mildred Jane at the Red Deer River ranch in 1903.

The decision to relocate was paying off. Grazing was good on the Red Deer River range, and John was steadily increasing his cattle herd and building up a horse-breeding business. His round-up skills were as much in demand on the Red Deer range as they had been at Sheep Creek. And he had won the respect of cowboys as far away as Medicine Hat. At the end of a round-up in 1903, John tried to check into the hotel in Medicine Hat. The desk clerk looked at the Black cowboy and refused to give him a room. A crowd of angry cowboys stormed the desk, and insisted that John Ware deserved the best room in the place.

It didn't take long for John to establish his reputation as a successful rancher. His neighbours along the Red Deer often asked for his advice. In 1904 an official from the federal department of agriculture came asking for his help. Cattle in Alberta were getting infested with mange mites, tiny creatures that caused an animal's hair to fall out in clumps. The condition weakened cattle so much that they were susceptible to cold and other diseases. The federal government had decided on a drastic cure. It had divided cattle country into 14 districts and wanted to set up a cattle dip in each one. The dip was a huge vat filled with a heated mixture of sulphur, lime, and water that killed the mange mites. The cattle went in one end and came out the other free of mites. The government official wanted to set up a cattle dip on John's ranch. John agreed, and his ranch became a centre in the fight against mange in Alberta.

Mildred Ware was just as busy as John. She was raising five (soon to be six) children, making clothes, milking cows, doing chores, managing all the bookkeeping, and running the ranch when John was out on the range. And he was the first to admit that the family's health and happiness and the success of the ranch was due as much to Mildred's efforts as his own.

In early Alberta, ranching women like Mildred carried incredible workloads. A bachelor homesteader wrote home: "I hope to marry—some young lady well versed in scrubbing, washing, baking, dairying, getting up at 3:30 in summer, 5:30 in winter, strong nerves, and strong constitution." He wasn't joking.

In their first year at the new house, a sixth child was born—Daniel, who was named after Mildred's father. It had been a difficult birth. Daniel was frail, and Mildred herself had been weakened by his birth. Daniel's health, the demands of caring for her other children, and the work on the ranch were all taking their toll on Mildred.

There were few doctors in early Alberta. Most of the time Mildred prepared her own home remedies to treat the family's ailments. Sometimes John was forced to make the long trip to Calgary to buy medicine for his children or his wife. In early 1903 John was getting more and more worried about Daniel and Mildred. His son required constant care, and Mildred was tired and weak.

In May, John boarded the train in Brooks. He was heading to Calgary to get medicine for Mildred. When he returned to

Brooks, he retrieved his horse from the livery stable and saddled up for home. Suddenly a spring blizzard hit with full force. People advised him to wait out the storm, but John was determined to get home to Mildred. He rode out of Brooks and into the storm. He had 40 kilometres to travel. After only a short distance, he realized his horse could go no further. He turned around and took the

A cattle dip similar to one built at John Ware's ranch.

horse back to the livery stable in Brooks, then he set out on foot. John plodded on, hour after hour. He struck a barbed wire fence that gave him some sense of where he was. He pushed on through the snow. Night came and still he forged ahead. Finally he saw a dim glow ahead. Mildred had put a lantern in the window to help John find his way home.

Despite the medicine and John's care, Mildred's health continued to fail. So did young Daniel's. He died early in 1905, just before his third birthday. Soon after, Mildred was admitted to hospital in Calgary. Her mother came to the ranch to care for the children. At the end of March 1905, a telegram arrived—Mildred Ware had died of pneumonia. John was devastated.

In his grief John had to face the question of what to do with his children. He decided to send them to their grandparents at Blairmore. He took on a hired hand, Pete Smith, a Black settler who had been working for the Lewises. John kept himself busy on the ranch, hoping to bury his sorrow.

As he immersed himself in work, John thought about how much he owed his wife. Mildred had overcome her shyness to marry a man more than twice her age. She had given up her interests in music and books to take on the hard life of a rancher's wife. She had supported his decision to move to the new ranch, even though she had loved the gentle hills at Sheep Creek. She had been a fine mother for his children and a lov-

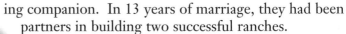

ing companion. In 13 years of marriage, they had been partners in building two successful ranches.

John had gained respect across the District of Alberta, but Mildred deserved her share of the credit. Years afterwards the organizers of the Calgary Stampede paid tribute to the pioneer women of cattle country: "It was these women who made it possible for the men to carry to success the undertakings they had commenced. No one thinks of those brave women who smiled through sickness, cold, loneliness, and poverty; few remember the great deeds they did in silence." These words could have been written about Mildred Ware.

John carried on ranching on the Red Deer River, but he was never the same. With his children living at Blairmore with their grandparents, he was lonely. Pete Smith, his hired hand, was a good man, but John missed his children. He asked the Lewises to send his oldest son, Bob, back to the ranch. He was only 11 years old, but John needed his company. He could also use Bob's help with the cattle herd, now numbering about 1,000 head.

On September 12, 1905, John and Bob were cutting out part of the herd. John was on his favourite horse, Flaxie. Suddenly she caught a foot in a badger hole. The horse went down and pinned John under her full weight. Bob rushed over to his father, but he wasn't moving. He galloped home to alert Pete Smith and then on to the nearest ranch to get help from Pete Eide. When Pete heard Bob's words, they chilled his heart: "It's dad. He's hurt bad." Pete and his son hitched their team to a wagon, thinking that they would carry John back to their ranch and fix him up. John Ware might be hurt, but in their minds he was indestructible.

The Eides followed Bob back to John. Flaxie stood with her head down, whinnying in pain. Pete Smith was looking down helplessly. John was lying flat on the ground, with his two large hunting hounds sniffing nervously around him. Pete Edie rushed over to John—one look was enough. He got Bob to call away the dogs. The Eides and Pete Smith lifted the big man onto the wagon and drove to Brooks. The news spread quickly—John Ware was dead.

John had worked as a cowboy for more than 25 years with-

Mildred Ware

out a serious injury. He had tamed some of the wildest broncs in the West without being thrown. He had ridden high-spirited cayuses across some of the roughest terrain on the open range. Yet he died riding a gentle horse on his own land.

The *Calgary Herald* reported the death of John Ware:

John Ware

> *Ware … an ex-slave from the south and for twenty-five years a rancher and cowhand in the west, owner of a thousand head of the finest range cattle on the Red Deer River, was killed today by a horse stumbling and falling upon him, killing him instantly. Deceased was 60 years old and leaves a family. Ware was one of the most widely known ranchers in this district. He was known as a roper and a rider and always won first money in any of the competitions he entered. He was a man of prodigious strength, and with apparent ease he could pick up an 18 months old steer and throw him ready for branding.*

The Eides arranged for John's body to be sent by train to Calgary. George Lane, who had purchased the Bar U in 1902, was in Brooks buying cattle when he heard of John's death. Lane took charge of the funeral arrangements in Calgary. John's old friend declared, "The best for this man is not good enough."

Cowboys and ranchers from across Alberta flocked to town to pay their respects. As the *Calgary Herald* reported, one of the founders of Alberta was gone: "The funeral of the late John Ware was held this afternoon. Rev. F.W. Paterson conducted the service and a great many from remote districts as well as townspeople were present to pay their respects to the remains of one of Alberta's pioneers."

At the funeral the pastor eulogized John as "a gentleman with a beautiful skin," respected by all. He recognized the racism that John had faced, but he spoke of how John's friends had judged him by his character, not by the colour of his skin.

More than 50 years after John's death, Joe Standish, who had worked for the Wares at Sheep Creek, spoke about the man who had more friends than he could count: "He was a fine man, John Ware."

Epilogue
Legend and Legacy

Inauguration Day ceremony in Edmonton. On September 1, 1905, Alberta became a province in the Dominion of Canada.

September 1, 1905—less than two weeks before John Ware died—was Inauguration Day for the new Province of Alberta. In Edmonton, Prime Minister Sir Wilfrid Laurier spoke to a cheering crowd of 15,000, many of them immigrants from the United States, Britain, and Europe. "We do not wish that any individual should forget the land of his origin," Laurier declared. "Let them look to the past, but let them still more look to the future."

John Ware had always looked more to the future than to the past. From the back of his horse, he saw things changing and moved ahead with the times. In the heyday of open-range ranching, he worked for two of the big ranch companies. Then the Canadian government changed its policy in the West— from one that encouraged cattle barons to set up huge ranches to one that encouraged settlers to establish family homesteads. So John gave up his old life as somebody else's ranch hand. He

60   *Legend and Legacy*

took advantage of the Dominion Lands Policy, homesteaded at Sheep Creek, and established a successful ranch with the help of his wife, Mildred. When he saw fences appearing on the Sheep Creek range and grazing land ruined by drought, John and Mildred sold their spread. They moved to the Red Deer River and built another successful ranch.

John seemed to know exactly when to move on or to change direction. He might have been considered a legend just for the wisdom he showed in reading his times. But he was known for much more—for his quiet determination, his physical strength, and his cowboy skills. For decades after his death, in bunkhouses and around campfires, Albertans told and retold stories of John's feats of strength and horsemanship. They told stories, too, of his loyalty, his generosity, and his kindness to fellow ranch hands and neighbours. Sometimes they twisted the tales to make John seem bigger than life. But a central truth remains in all these stories. John Ware was one of the best known and most widely respected figures in Alberta's early history.

Nettie, Arthur, Mildred Jane and Robert in 1966 in front of the statue of John Ware at the Horseman's Hall of Fame in Calgary.

A historical marker is located at the site of John Ware's Sheep Creek ranch near Millarville. His name lives on elsewhere in Alberta: Ware Creek, John Ware Ridge, Mount Ware, and John Ware Junior High School in Alberta. And visitors can see parts of John Ware's life and legacy on display at the Glenbow Museum and at Dinosaur Provincial Park.

John Ware

1845:	Born a slave in South Carolina
1863:	Becomes a free man with declaration of Emancipation Proclamation
1870s:	Travels to Texas to work as a cowboy
1879:	Drives cattle from Texas to Montana
1882:	Drives cattle from Idaho to the new District of Alberta
	Takes a job as a cowboy at the Bar U Ranch
1884:	Begins working at the Quorn Ranch
1885:	Registers his own cattle brand
	Patrols the High River range during the North-West Rebellion
1890:	Starts his own ranch at Sheep Creek
1892:	Marries Mildred Lewis
1900:	Moves to a new ranch on Red Deer River
1905:	Dies two weeks after Alberta becomes a province

Further Reading

Dempsey, Hugh A. *The Golden Age of the Canadian Cowboy: An Illustrated History*. Calgary: Fifth House, 1995.

Evans, Simon. *The Bar U and Canadian Ranching History*. Calgary: University of Calgary Press, 2004.

Evans, Simon, Sarah Carter, and Bill Yeo, eds. *Cowboys, Ranchers and the Cattle Business*. Calgary: University of Calgary Press, 2000.

Foran, Max. *Calgary: An Illustrated History*. Toronto: James Lorimer and National Museums of Canada, 1978.

High River Pioneers' and Old Timers' Association. *Letters from the Medicine Tree, 1960*. (Alberta Heritage Digitalization Project and University of Calgary, 2001: www.ourfutureourpast.ca/loc_hist)

Jameson, Sheilagh. *Ranchers, Cowboys and Characters: Birth of Alberta's Western Heritage*. Calgary: Glenbow Museum, 1987.

John Ware: *The Good Neighbour*. (video) Great North Productions, Inc., 1998.

Kelly, Leroy Victor. *The Range Men*. Toronto: W. Briggs, 1913.

MacEwan, Grant. *John Ware's Cow Country*. Edmonton: Institute of Applied Art, 1960 (repr. Vancouver: Greystone Books, 1995).

Macleod Bulletin.

Palmer, Howard, with Tamara Palmer. *Alberta: A New History*. Edmonton: Hurtig Publishers, 1990.

Smith, Barbara. *Passion and Scandal: Great Canadian Love Stories*. Calgary: Detselig Enterprises, 1997.

Acknowledgments/Credits

The author thanks the staff of the Glenbow Archives and Library for their assistance and the late Grant MacEwan for preserving in print the stories of the early cowboys and ranchers.

Library of Congress, Prints and Photographic Division: LC-DIG-ppmsca-04324 (p. 5); LC-USZC4-1526 (p. 6). Provincial Archives of British Columbia: A-03787 (p. 8). Glenbow Archives: NA-207-88 (p. 7); NA-207-74 (p. 8); NA-329-2 (p. 11); NA-117-1 (p. 12); NA-101-42 (p. 13); NA-967-41 (p. 14); NA-1939-2 (p. 16); NA-466-13 (p. 16); NA-1939-3 (p. 17); NB(H)-16-503 9 (p. 18); NA-237-16 (p. 19); NA-2245-1 (p. 20); NA-466-22 (p. 21); NA-2612-14 (p. 21); NA-237-20 (p. 22); NA-1480-11 (p. 25); NA-2382-2 (p. 25); NA-1654-1 (p. 26); NA-102-5 (p. 27); NA-660-1 (p. 29); NA-1365-1 (p. 30); NA-966-2 (p. 32); NA 239-25 (p. 33); NA-967-26, NA-1706-11, (p. 34); NA-156-10 (p. 35); NA-967-12 (p. 38); NA-4341-17 (p. 39); NA-262-2 (p. 42); NA 266-1 (p. 43); NA-468-15 (p. 44); NA-232-14 (p. 45); NA -263-1 (p. 46); NA-11812 (p. 47); NA-902-1 (p. 49); NA-3081-16 (p. 50); NA-266-3 (p. 53); NA-266-2 (p. 54); NA-266-4 (p. 55); NB(H) 16-460 (p. 57); NA-1297-4 (p. 60); NA-3165-108 (p. 61). Library and Archives Canada: Acc. No. 1946-110-1. Gift of Mrs. J.B. Jardine (p. 9); PA-066544 (p. 10); C-063257 (p. 40); C-05851 (p. 51). Parks Canada, Mildred Day Lane Estate Collection, 95.01.01.09 (p. 26). Manitoba Archives 269-1 (p. 37).

Index